The Secret Power of Lists

The Secret Power of Lists

By Deepak Rana

Neepradaka Press

Published by Neepradaka Press 2010
All rights reserved.

ISBN 978-0-9564928-0-7

Copyright (c) 2010 by Deepak Rana

Deepak Rana asserts the moral right to be identified as the author of this work.

All rights reserved. No part of this publication may be reproduced, stored in a retrieval system, or transmitted in any form or by any means, electronic, mechanical, photocopying, recording or otherwise, without the prior consent of the Publishers.

All images & Cover Image copyright (c) 2010 Deepak Rana

Acknowledgements

A big thank you to everyone who helped to make this book a reality.

A SPECIAL THANK YOU to my wife Deepti for her encouragement, love and support.

All quotes in this book come from the Bhagavad Gita

'The Wise see's knowledge and action as one; they see truly'

Contents

Preface		1
How to use this book		5
Materials Required		9
Chapter 1:	Lists-the Journey	17
Chapter 2:	List to Pass Exams	37
Chapter 3:	List to Get a job	47
Chapter 4:	List to Find a Partner	55
Chapter 5:	List for Health	65
Chapter 6:	Confidence Booster List	73
Chapter 7:	List to Increase the Flow of Money	81
Chapter 8:	List to Help Relationships	89
Chapter 9:	List for Sleep Problems	97
Chapter 10:	Lists- What Next?	105
	Further Reading	119

Preface

This book is a complete guide to getting everything you want in life by using the secret power of lists.

The lists have been used in certain regions of India, and either passed down within families, or to individuals by yogi's and other religious persons. It was the passing down of such a list (when I was facing exams), which began my research in to the lists, and in particular, the methods to correctly apply the lists, to bring about success.

Will lists work for you?

If you follow the methods outlined in this book, you will certainly get results. This is by large a practical book, and purposely written to be as easy to follow as possible. Try not to guess how the results may come to you, or how exactly your future will be different. Simply follow the method, and live in the present with the knowledge that the power of the list is working to help you. The Sanskrit words in the lists, have been taken directly from lists that are either in current use or have been obtained from a trusted source. They were copied by hand, photographed, and thereafter placed in this book. Indeed, the book you hold in your hands right now is vibrating at a certain energy due to the lists within the pages. Look after this book and make full use of it, as it has been written to be as practical and straightforward as possible, without dwelling so much on theoretical and metaphysical concepts. A reading list is provided at the back of the book if you wish to read further.

How to use this book

If you are in a hurry...

...to get started then read the materials required in the next section. Then browse through the contents and decide on what you want. You can skip the introduction part of any chapter and go straight to the essentials and method section. The lists are written in Sanskrit along with the translation, including an English transliteration of the word. This will help you to speak the words you write the list. The more lists you write, the easier it will become to write and speak them. Take your time and savour the words as you speak them. They truly sound beautiful when spoken out loud, and remember that these sounds have a vibrational energy which affects the physical world.

If you have more time...

...then read about how I began my journey in to discovering the secret of the lists. You may also be inspired by the true stories of people given in the introductory part of the chapters, who have used the lists successfully. They were able to harness the power of lists to make changes in their lives, and remember that you too can make the lists work for you. The final chapter 'List's, what next?', will assist you to look out for clues the universe is sending you to bring about success.

You may obtain the photofile of the lists for enlargement to enable clearer reading. Email me via neepradaka@gmail.com

Materials Required

Most of the materials you require for the lists will be easily obtainable, so great expense is not required to get started. Here I provide general advice on the common materials required. The essentials page in each chapter will provide further detailed information.

Pen

The lists will call upon you to use a pen, and it is recommended that you use your favourite pen. If you wish, you may decide to purchase a new pen to begin the lists. That is acceptable, as long as you continue to use the pen in other areas of your life. For example, if you complete an application form for a job, you will be asked to use the same pen when completing the list.

The choices of pen are numerous, and what you choose should feel comfortable for you to write with without too much discomfort. The ink should be smooth flowing, so as not to interrupt the flow of the writing. Avoid pens which do not have a suitable grip for the fingers. You will find that extended use of such a pen, will cause your fingers to slide down the barrel, and you will have to readjust every few words.

Paper

Lined paper is best. The most ideal size I have found is the U.K. A4 size (30x29inches). This will allow at least 5 sets of words on one side of the paper. If you wise to use a smaller size, be aware that you may end up using lots of paper, as some lists require more sets of words to be written. This can prove problematic if you are required to keep the sets of paper together and carried around with you.

Try and obtain good quality paper which will not allow ink to soak through to the other side. Some people use different types of papers from coloured, to parchment style. They will then draw pencil lines as a guide for their lists. The choice is entirely up to you.

Barriers

At first you will find it difficult mastering both the writing of the Sanskrit words and the reading of them. Your mind will give you all sorts of reasons to stop doing the lists, in order to avoid the initial hard work. Or you may have a subconscious barrier that is trying its best to stop you from carrying on with the list, and preventing you from success. It is important to acknowledge these barriers, but do not let them prevent you from moving forward. Everyone deserves to succeed and gain happiness in their lives, and you are no different. Yes it will be hard work at first, but as you push through each barrier, you will notice small changes within yourself which will propel you to succeed with the list, and to get a result. I have found this true in my own experience of using the list for exam success. Often I would tell myself that rather than do the list in the morning, I should do it later in the evening. That, I would be more relaxed in the evening and thus, be able to give my full attentions to the list. But then the evening would come, and I would come up with all kinds of excuses to avoid doing the list. This was my subconscious at play, which feared me succeeding and was putting in all kinds of blocks in my way to prevent me doing the list. Why would my subconscious be preventing me from succeeding? The answer is because the subconscious will do everything to prevent you from hurt, whether real or imagined. At some point in my life, I may have had thoughts about what would happen next after I had succeeded in my exams. I may have entertained fears that I would then need to go to college and be faced with further exams. I may have thought about the problems with moving away to college, and the fears of being alone and isolated, and having to meet new people. All these fears the subconscious would know about and thus come up with barriers to prevent these possible scenarios from occuring, by stopping me from succeeding in exams. That is why athletes will always try and visualise winning, and all of the positive beneficial effects of winning. By sweeping away all doubt, the athletes prevent their subconscious from creating barriers which would lead to poor performance. So how did I manage to overcome this barrier?

I got around it by putting an exact time in my diary of when I would do the list, and made a promise to myself that I wouldn't deviate whatever happened. This worked, although it was difficult to focus my mind on completing the list. I would think to myself that maybe after I have done one set of words, I will just have a quick cup of tea and return to the list after a few minutes. But I never allowed myself to take that break, until the full list was all done and completed. After a week, things settled down and it became a pleasurable experience to do the list. A month later I was actually looking forward to doing the list. I knew then, that some kind of internal barrier had been breached and I was starting to believe in myself, and that exam success was not some dream, but a reality that would be realized. Exam success for me meant getting certain grades in certain subjects, and in that I was successful. Exam success for another person might have meant top marks in everything. So when you judge the power of the list remember it will bring you what you determine as having been successful, not what others may consider is success. At the end of the day, what is important is that you get the results that make you happy, and bring you closer to your life goals.

'The Mind acts like an enemy to those who do not control it'

'Man is made by his belief. As he believes, so he is'

Lists- the journey

The journey began in India, whilst in conversation with a young boy on a train. He was a student on his way to college. I spoke of my nervousness of my school exams coming up in the next few months. I told him of the terror of it all, which was preventing me from focusing my mind on revision. He asked me whether I used lists, and thinking that he was talking about mnemonics, I explained I did not, and that I used simple notes. He looked back at me confused, and then opened up his backpack, taking out a notepad. In the back of the notepad were a few loose pages which he pulled out and showed me. It was a list written in what I assumed was Hindi, and I asked what the list was in revision for. He shook his head and explained that his grandfather had told him to make a list, which would help him study better and pass exams. I didn't think much about it at the time, and continued on my train ride.

I happened to mention the conversation to another relative later that evening, who it turned out took the use of lists seriously, and who went on to explain that there were lists used for other things as well. I was intrigued and that is where my journey began.

In the course of my further research I learnt about the use of lists in history and its mention in ancient Vedic texts. I speculated that perhaps these lists had evolved from spoken spells or prayers. Perhaps the process of writing them down in to lists, had made them more powerful. But why now were lists not as well known or used? It is perhaps not surprising as over time the methods can and do get lost in the passing down between one person to the next. Eventually the list may be lost, or survive but the methods in using them lost.

Consider that some common sayings we use today were used in relation to a particular method. But as things have evolved they are no longer associated with the original application of that saying:

Letting the cat out of the bag
Currently used when we accidently let slip a secret
Originally applied to when pigs sold in sacks and cats were put instead to trick people.

Basket Case
Currently used to define someone as mentally deficient.
Originally referred to wounded soldiers who had lost arms or legs and therefore had to be carried in baskets.

Break the ice
Currently means to break down social formality.
Originally applied to ships which were used to 'break ice'.

The list which I had seen the young student on the train using, was written in Sanskrit, and so was every list I discovered during my research. I found that those who did not understand Sanskrit, had learnt to copy the words, and had learnt how to speak them by the person who had passed down the list to them. They had then written a transliteration of the word in their native language, be it Hindi, Gujarati or Tamil. This assisted them to not only copy the Sanskrit words but to learn how to speak them. After using these lists for a couple of months, the persons became proficient enough to know how each word was spoken, without the use of the native language guide. Incidently it also helped that the many languages in India have their origins in Sanskrit, for example the word for examination (parikshaa) is the same in Sanskrit as it is in Gujarati.

One other thing which puzzled me was that some families were using different materials and yet getting the same success. For example in the case of the money list, some families were using a money box, some were placing coins in front of an idol of a particular God. I then realised that it worked because it was all reflecting the same symbolic thought of respecting and increasing money. In ancient times coins may have been given out to the poor as part of the method, or perhaps some other symbol of wealth was used such as rice or wheat. The important thing was that the correct thoughts and energies were created by the use of the object. I have therefore used the same idea for some of the methods in this book where there was a variation of the use of a particular object.

The Process of writing things down

Various texts have commented about the importance of writing down goals in order to achieve them. It is said to be a very powerful process, because the writing down of the goal provides a road map to follow. It allows the person to see where they want to go, and what they want to achieve in life. This allows the goals to be always within the mind, and to alert to the universe that this is what you want. It also signals to the inner mind to get working to turn the goals into reality.

This idea of goal setting is similar to a number of techniques that have gained popularity in recent times. It has been called by many names such as manifesting, cosmic ordering, universe ordering, quantum field vibration and so on. But they all have the main idea that one must write things down, focus on them, believe in them, and eventually the universe will bring about the changes desired. There have been countless stories of the success of these techniques, and bookshops have shelves full of such stories. There is a reading list at the back of the list if you would like to read further.

But what about the history of writing lists? Are they the same thing or something different? I believe the lists work in a similar way, but the main difference is the words and the methods which make them all the more powerful.

Sound vibration

Every sound made by the human voice-box carries with it a certain vibrational frequency, and in the Hindu tradition the universe is sound.

The world thus is created through sound at different frequencies and amplitudes.

Sanskrit is both a written and spoken language, and is the language used in Hindu prayers. The language was built up from the building blocks of sound, and therefore each letter became a representation of nature and the universe. Therefore, certain words were seen to connect with the universe and bring about various effects.

Vedic priests would speak Sanskrit prayers, and provide people with a 'mantra' which would be a certain sequence of words that would bring about a certain vibration within the universe. Sometimes yantra's would be made, which would be a number of Sanskrit words placed within a special 'grid'. These would be scribed onto metal plates such as copper, silver or gold as prescribed. These yantra's can still be purchased today in India as well as other Indian shops around the world. However the yantra's are generic ones produced for the mass market. Although they can still be effective, it is doubtful they can have the full power of a yantra that is custom made by a knowledgeable person, who has had the right training, and the right contacts. By the right contacts, it means with regard to persons in the metal-working trade where certain metals are required in specific amounts and transmuted in the correct way. A few photos of copper inscribed Yantra's can be seen on the following pages.

श्री बीसा यंत्र

।। लक्ष्मीयंत्र ।।

Cynatics

Work carried out by Ernst Chladni and Dr. Hans Jenny, demonstrated that various patterns could be made by sound on physical matter. This study of sound effects on physical matter is called Cynatics. Others have gone on to replicate these original experiments and created other newer ways of viewing sound effects on physical matter.

The use of the tonoscope for example has allowed the viewing of sounds as patterns on a screen. What is striking is that when letters of Sanskrit are spoken, they create the exact visual written Sanskrit symbol for that sound. The ancient symbol for Aum (see picture), can be seen on the tonoscope when spoken out loud. This provides evidence that the ancient language of Sanskrit, has its basis in the very fabric of nature. That when spoken we are able to affect nature. Sound can also affect our bodies. Considering the human body is made up of a large percentage of water, and that sound travels better through water, it stands to reason that sound can affect the human body. Some therapies have grown out of this discovery, to assist with all kinds of health problems. In medical science, ultrasound is used to destroy kidney stones. On the other side of the coin, some weapons have been created using sound as its method for disablement and death. For example ultrasound has been used to cause surface skin burns, and can be used to destroy internal organs, and Infra-sound can cause nausea.

Conclusion

So we have learnt about the Hindu tradition which see's the world as having been created through sound. We have also speculated about the origin of lists, and the power of writing things down. We have explored the physical nature of sound and its effects. All these combined together provides us with powerful evidence as to why the lists work to bring about change.

All there is left to do is to give them a try and see them become a reality in your life.

ॐ

'We are born into the world of nature; our second birth is into the world of spirit'

List to Pass Exams

Education has always been given high importance in Indian families. This list has been a popular one used by some Indian families, although its use has declined in favour of prayers, and other rituals prescribed by priests.

One family I spoke to used this list, however they did not have much faith in it, as some steps in the method had been lost in the process of passing it down. This seemed to be the case with quite a few families, and it was only through hundreds of contacts, that I was finally able to piece together the correct words and methods. I was then able to pass on the correct methods to those I had previously spoken to. Their success stories helped to prove that I had indeed found the correct method and words.

The list I have given will help focus the mind on your studies, and reduce the problems of procrastination and mind wandering. It will also help to reduce the general stress when revising for exams, and bring about a calmer, relaxed mind which will all be conducive to exam success.

Essentials

Pen: Your most used pen or the one you will be using in exams.
Good Quality Lined paper from your own study notepad.
Location: Whichever room you study the most in.

Method

Sitting in the room where you do most of your study, place a sheet of the lined paper in front of you.

With your pen begin by writing the words in the list.

This will count as one set. Start by writing another set beginning on the next line. You must complete ten sets and may turn the paper over to write on the back.

When you have completed ten sets, place the piece of paper either within your writing pad, your study folder, or in any book you carry around with you.

This procedure must be done one day every month until the end of your exams and all of the lists should be kept together.
After your exams are over you must gather all your lists and fold them into a small flat parcel and bury them beside any tree or plant in your garden. If you do not have a garden then purchase a large plant in which you can then deposit the lists (within the soil). If in the future you change the pot and need to use new compost, then you may dispose of the old soil by tipping it anywhere where plants are already growing (a park).

Sanskrit	Translation	Transliteration
परीक्षा	Exam	Pariksha
सिद्धि	Success	Siddhi
उतीर्ण	Passed	Uttirna
बोध	Knowledge	Bodha

'They all attain perfection when they find joy in their work'

List to get a job

Whether you are unemployed, or are wanting to change jobs, this list will help you every step of the way. It can also be used in conjunction with the confidence booster list, for when you get the job interview.
Some have reported that they have used this list for a particular job, which they really wanted, yet they didn't get that job. But soon after, an even better job had come their way, which they were successful in getting. So the main thing is to keep your eyes open for any opportunities that the universe brings your way. Apply to as many and varied jobs as you feel you may be capable of doing, and soon you will be rewarded.

Essentials

Two copies of the actual completed job application form you will be sending off (you can simply photocopy one). If you will be making an online application you should print off two copies of the completed application form.
The pen with which you completed the job application (or any pen if you made an online application)
Some lined paper
A time period of 24 hours allowance

Method

Place one application form to your left on the table and place your lined paper next to it, followed by the other application form next to that.

With your pen begin writing the following list on the lined paper.

This will count as one set. You must complete 10 sets in total and can use the back of the lined paper, or more sheets of lined paper if you run out of space.

When you have completed the sets, place the completed lists on top of one of the application forms and then place the other application form on top of that. In other words you are making a sandwich with the lists in the middle.

You must then leave these papers for at least 24 hours, and not touch or move them until the time has elapsed.

Once 24 hours has passed you can then send off the top application form. If it was an online application that has already been sent then go on to the next step.

Keep the list and completed application forms together in some place safe like a drawer. If you do not need the confidence booster, and will not be applying for any other jobs you must do the following.

Fold the list in half and either keep somewhere safe like the loft. If you will be applying for further jobs in the future you can take out this list and place a blank sheet on top to begin your new list. Keeping the old list and creating a new one will enhance its power. It is quite possible as you apply for more jobs in the future that you will accumulate a number of sheets whose power will be so very strong.

Sanskrit	Translation	Transliteration
जीविका	Employment	Jivika
सिद्धि	Success	Siddhi
यशि	Career	Cavita
वेतन	Salary	Vetana

List to Find a Partner

This list was originally used by Indian women to ensure they found a partner. However, it did not ensure that the partner would be the right one for them. It simply brought to them a lot of eligible people faster than the traditional way of waiting for a family to come with a marriage proposal. So this list will bring you lots of potential partners, but it will be up to you to find out more about them and decide whether they are the right person for you.

I found many happy couples who said they had used this list successfully to find the right person. For some of the cases it was hard to ascertain if it was just a happy coincidence. What proved to me that the list was successful, was in those cases where the individuals had been searching a long time for the right partner, and were only successful after they had begun the list.

There is the example of Jagina and Dinesh, both of whom had been trying many years to find a partner. The main difficulty was in their birth charts which they, and their families took very importantly when checking for potential marriage partners. It happens that some individuals are born in to a certain astrological sign, which means that they will only be happily compatible with another person, whose chart also shares a lot of the same aspects of the chart.

So both Dinesh and Jagina's parents had been trying their best to find the right person, to no avail for three years. Jagina had started to use the list near the third year, and Dinesh had been using the list for a slightly longer period.

They both believe their meeting was cosmically arranged. Dinesh found a new job in another city, and had moved there temporarily to see how things went. Part of his job meant he had to do a college course in the evenings. Jagina happened to be at the same college and had enrolled on the same course. This was on the advice of her father who felt that his daughter should get some qualifications, so that at least she could start working and gain some independence. Jagina later found out her father had almost given up hope of his daughter marrying, and felt that his daughter would be able to at least look after herself, if she ever were to remain single.

Well Jagina and Dinesh met at college and at first they both were reluctant to get to know each other better despite an attraction to each other. The attraction was so great that they would spend every breaktime together. Dinesh, however, felt he ought to explain about the astrological chart problem and put a stop to anything going further. It was then that Jagina explained that she too had the same sort of chart, and that maybe there was a reason they were drawn to each other. It didn't take long for both of the families astrologers to look over their charts and approve the union.

A lot of the meeting between partners I discovered, came about through strange coincidences and chance meetings. Often one or both partners had felt as if they were being gently guided along, and been given strength to overcome problems with shyness and other barriers to finding their partner. So with these stories cases in mind have a go at the list and see what happens in the next few months.

I have mentioned the use of the valentines card and a romance novel as a token of love as it is readily available, and in a format that is easy to use. In India other items are used instead such as wheat or rice grains which signified fertility.

Essentials

A pen you usually use

A symbol of love (Valentines card) –You can purchase from a shop if available or you can print one off online. The best would be to create your own card with your own design and wording. Whichever card you choose must be the kind of card you would like to receive.

A good quality piece of lined paper

A book about love: A romance novel is ideal, or you can use this book.

Method

Begin by writing in your name in top area of the valentine card as if the card had been given to you. The envelope can be discarded.

Place the lined paper on top of the valentines card and begin writing the list

This will count as one set. Complete a total of 20 sets, and you may use the back of the paper, and additional pieces of paper.

Once complete, fold the lists in half and put them inside the card. The card can now be placed inside your book.

The book must then be placed somewhere safe where it will not be moved for one month. After one month, if you are still unsatisfied with either the number or quality of the type people coming into your life, you may repeat the procedure using another sheet of lined paper. You may continue this the following month, for up to a year, or until you have found a partner

Sanskrit	Translation	Transliteration
भाविक	Soul	Bhaavika
समागमन	Union	Samagamana
चित्ति	Heartfulness	Citta
प्रमोद	Joy	Pramoda
हास	Laughter	Haasa

List for Health

The list here was used in conjunction with various ayurvedic medicine and practices. As ayurveda medicines grew in popularity, the use of lists became less significant. It is still prescribed as part of a full ayurveda treatment at some places in India. The list provided here is a generic one which will work for any health problem. In most cases however a specific health problem will require a specific list. But, to provide them in this book would mean having a number of lists which would run into hundreds of pages.

Essentials

A pen
One piece of lined paper

Any single piece of information relating to your health problem. This can be a prescription, or a single print out from the internet of the health problem. In India a note from a doctor is used. You can not use anything you have written yourself (such as a typed written document about your illness, or a printout of an email you have sent to someone mentioning your illness).

Method

Begin by placing your lined paper on top of the paper relating to your health problem.

Start writing the list which will count as one set. You must complete 20 sets in total. Once complete take one page of the completed list and fold into a small parcel. This should be kept close to you either in a pocket or wallet.

The other lists along with the health information paper should all be folded in half and kept near any plant. It is preferable if it is kept near a Tulsi plant. Tulsi has a special significance within India both spiritually and physically. The Tulsi plant is venerated, and its leaves and other parts of the plant are used in ayurvedic medicines.

Sanskrit	Translation	Transliteration
शक्ति	Energy	Zakti
देह	Body	Deha
निरामय	Health	Niraamaya
उद्धार	Repair	Udhaara
स्तास्नु	Stable	Staasnu
तेजते	Energise	Tejate

Confidence Booster

There are many times in life where an extra boost in confidence is required. This list is perfect for such situations. It can be used on the day of a job interview, a first date, first day on a job, or when having to speak to someone over an important issue. Whichever situation it is, this list will give you that extra bit of help. In India this was mostly used when attending an important meeting. For example a meeting requiring a loan, or by a young man or woman in the course of marriage arrangements.

Essentials

Your favourite pen
One piece of lined paper (possibly two)
This book (to represent achievement)

Method

This list is to be completed the day before the confidence boost is required.

Write out the following words on the piece of paper, using the other side if necessary. You must complete 5 sets. Once complete, fold in half and place the paper on this page of the book.

The book must then be taken with you wherever the confidence boost is needed. So you may keep it in your bag when going to the job interview. If there is no possible way for you to take the book with you, then you must make a duplicate list. Keep the one list inside the book on this page and leave at home. The other list should be kept folded and put into a pocket close to the body.

In India these are sometimes folded up and kept in a small metal locket worn by both men and women. They vary in size from square sized to cylindrical ones. Generally they will hold pieces of paper with a 'spell' given to them by a guru to give the person good luck, to ensure they don't have accidents, or to avoid the evil eye.

Sanskrit	Translation	Transliteration
शक्ति	Energy	Zakti
देह	Body	Deha
निरामय	Health	Niraamaya
उद्धार	Repair	Udhaara
स्तास्नु	Stable	Staasnu
तेजते	Energise	Tejate

Increasing the Flow of Money

Most people want to have more money. This list will gradually increase the flow of money coming into the home. There are a number of reasons why money has either reversed it flow, or stopped altogether. What this list will do is work on reducing the factors causing the negative reversal, and then eventually build up enough momentum to move in a positive direction.

I can cite the case of one family living in an affluent area of Surat. The house looked newly built, with some building site workers still making some finishes to garden wall. I met the owner of the house, Kishen, and his family and was offered lunch at a restaurant, with the architect with whom the Kishen was explaining some other things he wanted done to the house.

The architect then left us to go elsewhere and I brought up the subject of my visit. Kishen explained that where the house now was, there was a much smaller building comprised of only three rooms. That building then, was used as a shed and was an outbuilding belonging to the much larger house next to it. The owner of that house had put the house on rent. Thus when Kishen came from the village to the city and found work, he was able to rent this shed and then bring his wife to live with him. He had got work at the local newspaper factory, and made his money labouring within, and then selling the papers out on the streets until late evening.

For a year the couple and their new born daughter were able to live a somewhat comfortable living. But then things changed and they found that they were falling short of money every month to pay the rent, even though there had been no rent increases. Money seemed to be flowing away from them. Every month something came up which required paying someone. It then happened that they were choosing whether to eat two, or one meal a day. Some days Kishen said he would lie and say he had eaten for free at the factory, just so his wife and daughter could eat properly. Not being able to afford the rent, they were forced to pack up and leave the city for the village parental home. Things were equally hard there, as the reliance on crops for money was diminishing. Then, one day, a yogi was travelling through the village, and happened to stop by the house to ask for some water. It is traditional to offer food and water to such people and so Kishen's wife prepared a small meal with what they had. The sage then told them to take a leaf which he took from his cloth bag. On it were written some Sanskrit words in yellow tumeric. The sage then spoke the words, and explained that they should write these words on a leaf and speak them every day. In addition they were to deposit a coin onto the leaf every time they spoke the five words on the list. The coins could be used after the list was complete. He assured them that their lives would change for the better. After the sage left, Kishen was skeptical and asked his wife not to bother. But his wife told him she would do it as they had nothing to lose from it. One month later the neighbouring landowner asked Kishen if he wanted to buy his field as he could not work it anymore. All he asked was that he be left to live in his house. Kishen said he could not afford the land and no-one would be willing to give him a loan. His neighbour then came by the following day to say that he knew of someone who would offer a loan. That same day Kishen obtained a loan and was became owner of a large piece of good field land. Along with his wife he raised a crop which brought immediate profits. Eventually he hired people to work the land, and was able to earn enough to purchase yet more land. Within a year of his wife starting the list he was a well off family able to take vacations and purchase houses for renting out. It just so happened that he saw the shed for sale in the city which he had rented years ago. This was being sold along with the larger accommodation, and Kishen purchased it immediately and set about to knock it all down so he could build the house of his dreams. So, he said, something changed the moment his wife started the list. The universe had poured on him abundant opportunities for success. I asked if his wife still did the list to which he replied with a smile 'we both do. But now we use paper and pen instead of leaf and tumeric paste'.

Essentials

Some lined paper
A pen
A money box (anything with a slot that can hold coins)

Method

Write out the list which will count as one set.

Everytime you complete one set, place one coin in the money box.

Once you have completed ten sets fold one piece of paper small enough to be able to slot into the money slot of the money box. The other piece of paper should folded into a square and kept in a pocket as close to your body as you can. This will ensure that wherever you go opportunities to flow money towards you will reveal themselves and also allow you to recognize them and take action.

You may wish to use the coins in any transaction once they have been entered in to the moneybox.

Sanskrit	Translation	Transliteration
धान	Money	Dhana
आधिक्य	Abundance	Aadhikya
तटिनी	River	Tatinii
अयस्कान्तीय	Magnetism	Ayaskaatiiya

List to Help Relationships

This list is specifically for couples. If you are experiencing ongoing troubles within your relationship, then this list will help. It will assist in getting to the cause of the problems, and bring about possible ways forward. It will also provide emotional strength to cope with whatever developments take place.

I met Geeta at a café. A bubbly person who came across as very confident in herself. She was now working as an investment banker for a national bank. I was intrigued with what list she was using. One for wealth, job success or confidence? She revealed all in the next hour of conversation. She told me as was traditional in her and in many families in India, that her marriage was arranged and that she had met her prospective husband only once before the wedding, and being extremely shy she had no courage to ask any questions. One thing he did tell her was that they would living alone, and not within a large family home as is the norm. This provided some relief as the new bride is often burdened with pleasing the other members of the family, by doing all the housework and so on. Living apart would mean she would be able to focus on her husband and would provide a good base to get to know each other.

Alarm bells rang in the first week of marriage when she asked her husband when he was going back to work. He told her he didn't have a job but was hopeful he would get one. He would then go out every evening saying he was going to ask about jobs, but would return late at night drunk. The second week she plucked up the courage to ask him to refrain from going out each evening leaving her alone. That was the first time he hit her. Geeta then recounted a number of similar incidents that led to beatings. He also forced himself upon her that she fell pregnant. However she lost the baby after an incident of brutal beating. Convinced he would one day kill her she ran away back to her parental home. Her parents could not bear the shame of having a daughter return home, so they sent her to live in secret with her grandmother. It was her grandmother who told her about the list to help with relationships. Eventually her husband found her, and asked her back to live with him, saying he would behave, and so she agreed. But a week later he was back to his old self. Geeta began the list, sometimes writing in physical pain after a beating. A week later the police came at the door saying they had heard reports of the husband beating the wife. They warned him that they were watching him and it worked. Now Geeta's husband stayed out most nights returning only in the late afternoons where he would sleep. On those rare nights where he did return to the house, he stayed away from Geeta. Geeta eventually found a job during the day which at least gave her some income to purchase essential items. Her husband then began to stay away for days, then return for a day or two before going missing again. Then he was missing for a week which turned into a month. Geeta started attending school after finding out about adult courses from a poster. There she met other people who offered her advice and guidance. She filed for divorce and her husband was eventually traced, living rough, who didn't object to the divorce. Geeta gained some qualifications and in a short time made her way up to a senior position within a bank. She found new friends, and had learnt to believe in herself and to take charge of her own life. She eventually found a life partner whom she says is her true soul mate.

Essentials

Lined paper
Your favourite pen
Two objects: One belonging to yourself and another belonging to your partner. Anything small will do, such as a button or a ring.

Method

Place the piece of paper in front of you, with the two objects together on the page.

Begin writing out the list. This will count as one set. A total of ten Sets should be completed. After completing the list, you should fold them in half and keep them somewhere safe where they will not be disturbed. The objects can be either returned or kept to one side for the next day. You can continue with the list for as long as necessary, and keep placing the lists in the same place as the other lists.

Sanskrit	Translation	Transliteration
शक्ति	Power	Zakti
सिद्धि	Barrier	Rodha
समागमव	Union	Samaagama-
उद्धार	Repair	Udhaara

List for Sleep Problems

The list here will bring about a restful mind, which will aid peaceful sleep. So whether you have always had trouble sleeping, or whether it has become a recent problem, this list will help.

It is also important that you also look at other factors which may be playing a part in your sleep troubles. For example the placement of the bed, the distance of electrical devices and so forth can all be causing problems for you.

The list here calls for the use of a small piece of rose quartz. The stone will be able to harness the power of the list and aid restful sleep when placed under the pillow. Therefore find a piece that is small enough not to cause discomfort when placed under the pillow. Stones such as quartz are used extensively in India, placed in rings, or worn as jewellery. They are used mainly to aid in overcoming the negative aspects of certain planets, based upon an individuals particular astrological chart. But they can also be used in general for health benefits. Further reading about the use of rocks and crystals can be found in the reading list at the back of the book.

Essentials

Lined Paper
Pen
A small piece of rose quartz

Method

Place the piece if paper in front of you and place the rose quartz at the top of the paper. Begin to write the words in the list. This will count as one set. Complete 5 sets in total making sure you speak the words slowly so the sounds vibrate within you and the quartz.

Place the list under your pillow along with the piece of quartz. As a further aid to sleep you may read the list before going to bed. It is important for you to speak the words. Read the list as many times as you can before you feel sleepy.

You can continue with the list until peaceful sleep is restored. This should bring results in two months, and so if problems persist it may be worth looking at the other factors affecting sleep. These were touched upon at the beginning of the chapter.

Sanskrit	Translation	Transliteration
शान्ति	Peaceful	Zaanti
रजनि	Night	Rajani
शान्त	Calm	Zaanta
शम	Restful	Zama

Lists...What next?

So, you have been writing the lists and wondering, what next. This chapter has been written to assist with looking out for signals from the universe, which are there to guide you along the path towards your goal. I will provide some real life examples from people who have used the lists, and the various ways the universe has guided them towards success. By illustrating the numerous ways the universe can guide, you will be better placed to discover and take advantage of instances in your life where the universe is speaking to you.

Dreams

You may find that a week or so after doing a list that you are getting dreams that are different than is the norm for you. For example, some people have said that they have been able to recall their dreams much more easily than before, and that their dreams have become more vivid. Let me tell you about Mahesh who had been suffering a lot from painful urination for a couple of months. He had gone to his doctor many times and was prescribed various medicines for urine infections. These did not work and he continued to live in pain. He was advised by friends to seek Ayurvedic treatments but he was highly sceptical of them and preferred to stick with his doctor. The pain gradually got worse, and was preventing him getting a proper nights sleep, and was affecting his work at the bank. He had enough by then, and was willing to try anything. It was the mother of a friend who heard about his troubles, and passed on the health list for urinary problems. Mahesh began the list and a week later there was still no relief in his pain. On those occasions where he was able to get some sleep he would get vivid dreams. He described his dream to me,

'I was standing on a beach looking up at the sky which was bright blue. I then noticed red coloured circles of light which were starting to dance in the sky. I was laughing at how these red circles were dancing, they looked so funny. Then I would feel a sudden feeling of sadness and emotional pain and the red circles were starting to grow darker in colour. A green coloured circled appeared and started to absorb the red circles one by one. Each time a red circle was absorbed I felt such sadness, the kind of which I have never experienced and I would wake up in tears.'

This dream replayed itself many times to Mahesh. Sometimes the location would be different, for example he might be standing in a street looking at the sky. Sometimes he would be looking at water in which the red circles were dancing. Then one morning, whilst he was getting ready for work he noticed the play of the morning sun causing circles of light to reflect off a glass, causing dancing circles on the wall. One of the circles was red and it was dancing around his telephone diary. As Mahesh went to take a closer look the diary dropped on the floor and it opened up on his doctor's page. Something in him then compelled him to make a call to his doctor to ask if he had any further news on helping with his problem. His doctor said no, but then asked him to come and see him that same day just for checkups.

At the surgery Mahesh was laid down on the doctor's bed as the doctor proceeded to examine his abdomen. Mahesh's eyes fell upon a poster for tuberculosis. There was a circle of red representing a red blood cell and other circles representing other cells. It reminded him of his dream. Involuntarily Mahesh spoke the words 'tuberculosis', to which his doctor shook his head and said T.B. was generally something to do with the lungs.

Mahesh pushed the doctor further, and convinced him to send off his urine samples for testing of TB. A week later Mahesh got the call from his doctor telling him that Mahesh had got T.B. in his kidneys.

It was rare for it to occur in kidneys, and that it wasn't the norm to ask for T.B. checks from a urine sample. It was treatable with a course of antibiotics for at least six months. Finally Mahesh had got an answer for the health problems afflicting him. The universe had guided him to find the answer through his dreams. Mahesh continued with the list until he was free of all pain and tests confirmed the T.B. bacterium had gone from his body.

Sometimes dreams can be up front and direct as in the case of Jennifer. Jennifer had left college for a year, and had since been looking for a job. She had graduated in accountancy but her heart wasn't in it as a profession for her. However she still was applying for jobs within the field. Whilst researching this book I sent off the chapter on finding a job for her to have a try. I had an email two weeks later, an extract as below,

'I want to tell you I have found a job that I love and feel like this is what I should be doing in life. It's so weird, how it happened. The first night when I did the list I had a dream where I was walking past a shop selling Teddy Bears, and every time I would be standing outside looking at the display. The teddy bears in the display all looked worn and dull and I was thinking to myself how on earth would they sell any bears with a display like that. Then in my dream I would be conjuring up all kinds of different teddy bear display arrangements. This same dream happened again, for the next four nights, and I probably ended up with over 50 different teddy bear display arrangements!. Here's the strange thing. My friend asked me to give her a lift to town and whilst there I passed a teddy bear shop in the mall. Their display was empty with only a poster in the window. I ventured into the shop and felt like I was on autopilot. I asked the person at the counter what happened to the display and she said they never had one before. I then went on to tell her how good a display would look. I was so enthusiastic about it all that she convinced me to come back and explain my ideas to the area manager. She also told me that the store was pencilled to be closed down due to low sales and the shop manager had even left a few months early to find another job. Next day I met with the area manager and after listening to me for 20 minutes going on about teddy bear displays she asked if I wanted to work for her as the shop manager, just until they closed the store in a few months. Next day I was working as a shop manager! I cleared out all the posters in the window and setup my first teddy bear display based on one in my first dream. That same day we had so many customers coming in I had to phone the area manager for extra staff. I love my job so much and this week I had a call to say that the sales figures have tripled in a week and its rank has jumped from last place to the top ten of all the chains. They are not going to close the shop and next week I have a meeting to discuss my promotion to area marketing manager! A result after a few days with the list, I never thought something like those would work so fast'

Sign-people

This is a term which I use to refer to the appearance of certain people which prove to be highly beneficial to the list-writers goal. They may be people you know, or total strangers. Some say the strangers are Deva's (angels), and there is a lot of literature concerning people who claim that angels have been sent to them to protect in times of need. Others claim that everyone has a Guardian angel, who is always around and will come to peoples aid when asked. Whoever these sign people are, in the context of the lists they play an important role on behalf of the universe as the following accounts illustrate.

A married couple, Karanjit and Parminder, had started to have problems two years into their marriage. It began with short arguments over little things which gradually grew into loud shouting fights, leading to prolong periods where they would not speak to each other. As Parminder said, 'we both felt like a dark cloud had come over us and we were both depressed all the time'. Karanjit was spending more time away from home, he says 'I would use any excuse to not go home as I knew that once I got home, something would trigger another fight. I think we both knew it was silly to fight over little things but we just couldn't stop'. They happened to be at the temple on one occasion where there was a visiting yogi who was inviting people to speak to him with any problems and issues. It was Karanjit who went to the yogi and was given a list. 'It was unusual to be given a piece of cloth with some words on it' Paramjit said, 'usually yogi's would give a mantra to be spoken secretly, or a piece of fruit that had been energised for us to eat'.

They both began the lists, and after the first week they felt something was changing, 'my mind just felt more cooler and things that used to irritate me before had no effect on me' says Parminder. They still had arguments however, but only once a week rather than every day. This continued for another month. In the third month the couple were walking in the park on the way home from a relative's house. There in the park they say they met what they believe to be a Deva (angel). He was walking towards us, and he seemed to have his eyes set upon us. He stopped and asked us where we were off to. Then he started to ask us where we were from, and within us both we felt this urge to tell him everything about us. After this, he told us to continue with our journey and walked off. Paramjit says that 'I was feeling like I was glowing as if I had been thirsty and had drank some sweet water'. Karanjit felt similar things, 'afterwards I felt like I wanted to just laugh out loud to the world in joy. It was if I had wanted to just talk and let things out and I had done it'.

Back at home they started to talk about the experience, and what they had talked to the Deva about, 'as we started to talk to each other I started to feel stronger connections to my husband. I started to see his way of seeing the world'. Equally Karanjit said 'it was like I was discovering things about my wife I had never known before. I could feel her pain from things I had inadvertently done or said in the past'. The Deva had opened up a healing communication channel between them, and the marriage started to get stronger, healthier and happier. 'The list began it all and the Deva I believe was sent to help us on our way' Paramjit said with a smile.

One salesman met a Deva that would change his fortune. Dharmesh was a seller of spare parts for bicycles. He would travel up and down Mumbai supplying shops with spare bicycle parts. It brought in enough money for himself, wife and two children to live on. But it was a very haphazard form of income, as some months would bring in low amounts of money, and other months he might do better. He began the list for money that was given to him by his wife, who had been given it by her parents when she had left home to start life with her husband. She had never gave it much thought and only happened to remember it by chance one day.

Soon after starting the list Dharmesh was on the train making his way home. It was late so the train wasn't as full as it normally is, and he noticed an elderly man who was looking intently out of the open window. The man then got up and walked towards Dharmesh and stood there. Dharmesh assumed the man's train stop was coming up. The elderly man then spoke and asked if Dharmesh knew where Sion was. Dharmesh knew where it was but he told the man that this train did not stop go there directly. He would need to get off at the next stop and then get a rickshaw to Sion.

The man looked worried and said he had no money, and whether it was a walkable distance. Looking at the elderly man Dharmesh could see he would find it difficult to walk any distance, and Sion was not walkable. 'I will take you there' Dharmesh said without thinking and the elderly man smiled and thanked Dharmesh.

When they got off at the stop Dharmesh called a rickshaw, and they set off to an address which the elderly man gave. When they reached the destination the elderly man thanked Dharmesh and then pointed to some buildings where he lived, and then to a much bigger set of buildings which he said was a technology college. As the man walked off Dharmesh noticed the number of bicycles that were parked inside the sheds of the college. They numbered into the hundreds and Dharmesh realised this maybe an opportunity.

The next morning Dharmesh returned to the same place, and was proved right, as he saw scores of children coming to college on bicycles. Dharmesh wondered what the other bicycles were doing last night parked in the sheds.

Dharmesh went into the school and found out that the school had purchased hundreds of bicycles to hire out to students. The school even had its own bicycle workshop, which repaired and maintained the bicycles. It turned out that the school was having problems maintaining the bicycles, as most of the time the mechanics time was being spend in going some distance to get spare parts. Right then Dharmesh struck a deal to supply parts to the school. Over time Dharmesh started to supply other things like stationary, disposal cups, and cleaning materials. He was able to purchase a small van, and even started to employ an extra person to help him with all of the workload.

Dharmesh is convinced the old man had been a Deva as he couldn't track him down, despite asking as many people in the area. He even spoke to the rickshaw driver who claimed that Dharmesh had been alone that night, and could not ever recall having two people in his rickshaw.

Out of time-slips

An Out of time-slip is something I use to describe moments which cause a person to feel they have stepped out of time. When such a slip happens they will have no sense of time passing, and it will be as if time does not exist. This is not the same as feeling that time has stopped, because at such moments one still has some feeling of time to know that time has stopped. In an out of time slip, the person will feel no effect of time and it will be as if they have never known 'time' as a concept.

This kind of slip will sometimes be the universe signalling to the person that something very important is happening, and that it needs to be acknowledged. I will provide a few short examples from true accounts of out of time slips by people who were doing a list.

Meeta was doing a list for exam success, and whilst studying she was getting an out of time-slip whenever she would read around a particular part of a book. She describes it as 'reading without really reading'. I asked what she meant and she explained that 'everytime I was reading a particular chapter I felt drowsy but I was still reading, and it felt like it was someone else reading, and I was listening in. When I got to the end of the chapter I realised that an hour had passed yet I didn't have any sense of time whilst reading'. I asked if she re-read the chapter a second time and if it happened again. She replied it only occurred once a day and only when she read around that particular subject in any book. Everytime it happened she said, she had to reread that chapter and she was getting frustrated about it. 'I started to feel less confident about my other subjects as I was rereading so much on the subject that was causing me the problem'. It proved very useful as it turned out the exam was heavily focused on that very subject, and Meeta could not believe her luck when she saw the exam paper. 'If it hadn't been the fact that I had reread so many times around that subject-I wouldn't have been able answer as well as I did'. She passed with 100 percent marks.

Another case is that of Neha, who was having difficulties in finding the right partner and was using the lists to help. She was at sat at wedding function when her eyes fell upon a man sat some distance away within a crowd of other people, and as she looked at him she had an out of time-slip. She was quite surprised when she dropped back into time that people were starting to head away towards the dinner hall, as to her it was only mid morning. On checking her watch, she saw an hour had passed by and she had not realised it. In the dinner hall Neha saw the man again in the waiting line and despite her shyness she felt she had to speak to him. She found an opportunity and managed to get a seat next to him at the dinner tables. The happy ending is that they got married a few months later. If it hadn't been for the out of time slip, Neha would never have thought about making any efforts to speak to the man.

Pretesh kept getting out of time-slips whenever he walked past a particular store selling jewellery. It was on his route to work, and to avoid it would mean walking a slightly longer distance. He was doing a list to help with his sleeping problems. The problem was not falling asleep, but waking up every night from nightmares. He had tried all he could think of to help, as well as getting advice from other people. He started the list with little hope that they would help.

So why was he getting out of time slips by a jewellery shop? Well, on one occasion he got no reaction at all when he passed the shop and Pretesh was curious why. He stepped into the shop, and browsed around. One of the salesmen approached him, and said they were having a special discount week, and whether Pretesh wanted to see a few items. Prestesh's eyes fell upon an inexpensive ring with a stone set inside it, which he purchased and went on his way home.

That night Pretesh had an uninterrupted night's sleep. Thinking it to be a one off, Pretesh didn't believe such a night would happen again but it did. The only thing Prestesh that had changed was that he was now wearing a ring to bed. So how could a ring be responsible for a good night's sleep? It may have been that Pretesh was waking up due to some internal problem, and the ring brought about a change in his energies, which relaxed his mind enough to give him a proper night's sleep free of nightmares. The slip was the universe's way of guiding him to a solution to his sleep problems.

So, as you have read there are numerous ways the universe may guide you towards what you want. Keep your eyes, ears, and heart tuned in and you should become skilled enough to recognise signs from the universe. I would love to hear more success stories and suggestions so please contact me via the publishers at: Neepradaka@gmail.com

You can also use this contact if you wish to get free photo images of the lists. These can be printed in large sizes to aid with clearer copying of the Sanskrit words.

May your dreams become reality

Further Reading

The following are a selection of books that expand some of the theoretical aspects that are touched upon in this book.

Hinduism

Bhagavad Gita-As it is
A.C. Bhaktivedanta Swami Prabhupada

Hinduism: A very short introduction
Kim Knott

The Essentials of Hinduism
Swami Bhaskarananda

Sanskrit

Teach Yourself Sanskrit
Richard Gombrich & James Benson

A Sanskrit Reader
Charles Rockman Lanman

An Essential Guide to Sanskrit
Dewnnis Waite

Cymatics

Cymatics: A study of Wave Phenomena & Vibration
Hans Jenny

Water Sound Images
Alexander Lauterwasser

The Cosmic Octave
Hans Cousto

Mantra

Healing Mantra's
Thomas Ashley-Farrand

Gayatri Mantra
S. Viraswami Pathar

Goal Setting

What are your Goals?
Gary Ryan Blair

Goals! How to get everything you want
Brian Tracy

Goals: Setting and achieving them
Zig Ziglar

Deva's or Angels

Deva Handbook
Nathaniel Altman

How to Hear your Angels
Doreen Virtue

Guardian Angels
Joan Wester Anderson

Synchronicity

Synchronicity:An Acausal Connecting Principle
Jung, C.G.

Crystals

Crystal Prescriptions
Judy Hall

Healing Crystals
Michael Gienger

Complete Guide to Manifesting with Crystals
Marina Costelloe

Sleep Problems

Electromagnetic Fields and Radiation: Human Bioeffects
Aiadh Habash

Electromagnetic Fields
Blake Levitt

Toxic Bedrooms
Walter Bader

Ten Natural Ways to Good Night's Sleep
Nikos Linardakis

Sound weapons

Future Weapons
Kevin Dockery

High Power Electromagnaetic Radiators
D.V. Giri

Future War: Non-Lethal weapons in 21st Century Warfare
John B. Alexander & Tom Clancy

B

Made in the USA
Lexington, KY
05 January 2011